一柳 慧

ティンパニのための

リズム・グラデーション

TOSHI ICHIYANAGI
RHYTHM GRADATION

for timpani

SJ 1104

SCHOTT

ティンパニのための《リズム・グラデーション》は、菅原淳の委嘱によって作曲され、1993年4月22日、朝日生命ホール（東京）で、菅原淳によって初演された。

演奏時間——11分

Rhythm Gradation for timpani was commissioned by Atsushi Sugahara. The first performance was given by Atsushi Sugahara on April 22, 1993 at Asahi Seimei Hall in Tokyo.

Duration: 11 minutes

SYMBOLS

(>)　　= Mild accent

✕　　= Strike the metal part on the edge

━(●)━　= No attack glissando within reverberation

♮　♭　= 1/4 tone higher

♮　= 1/4 tone lower

Rhythm Gradation
for timpani

Toshi Ichiyanagi

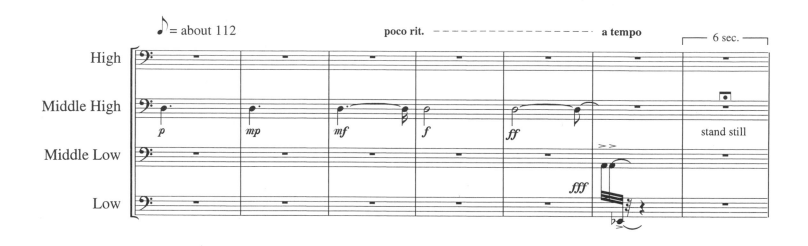

4

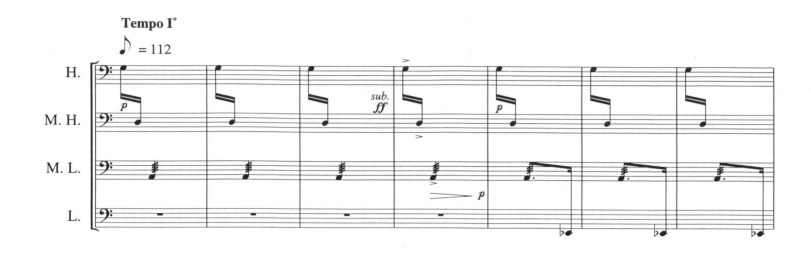

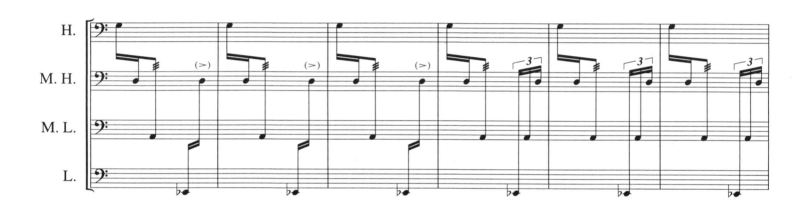

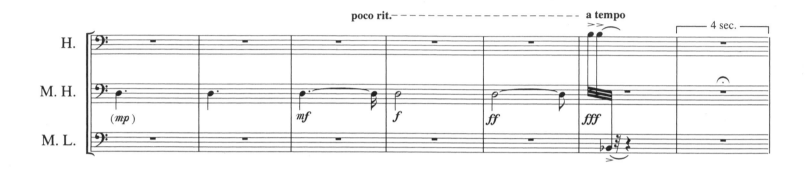

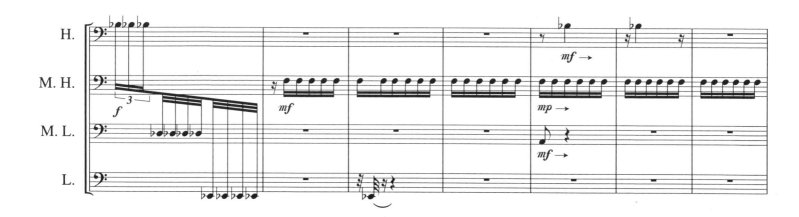

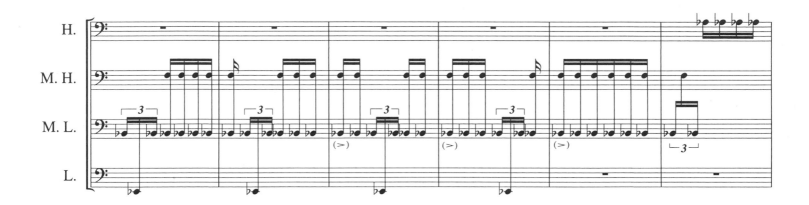

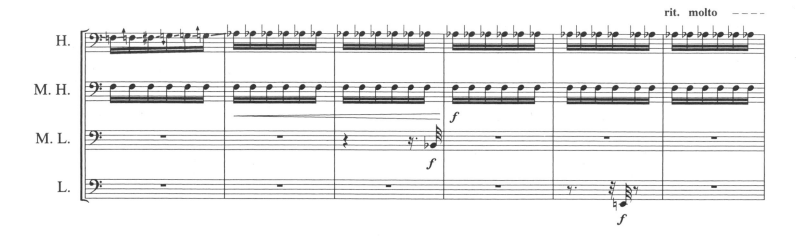

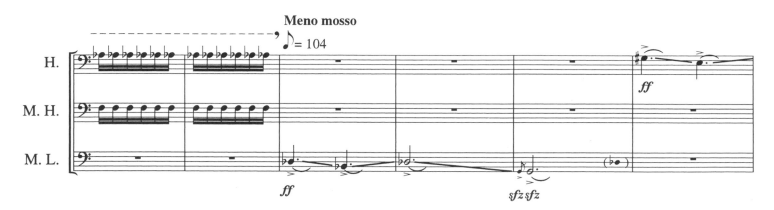

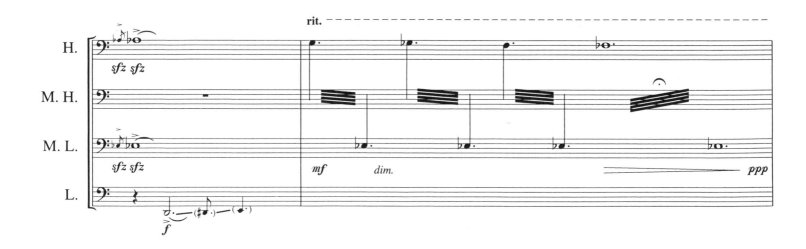

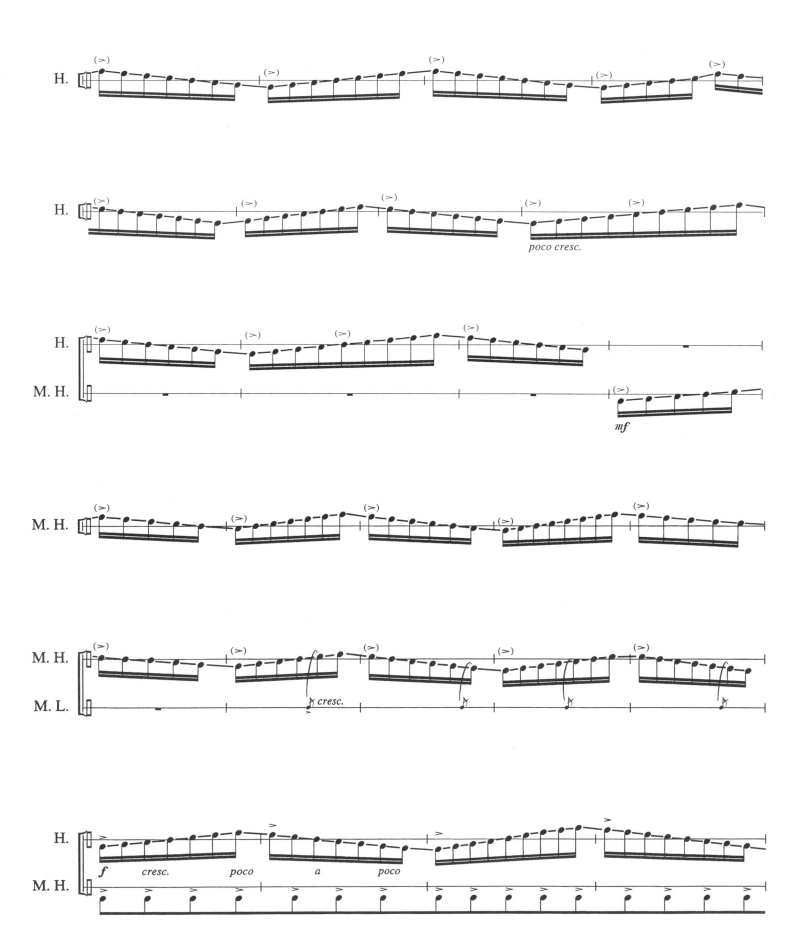

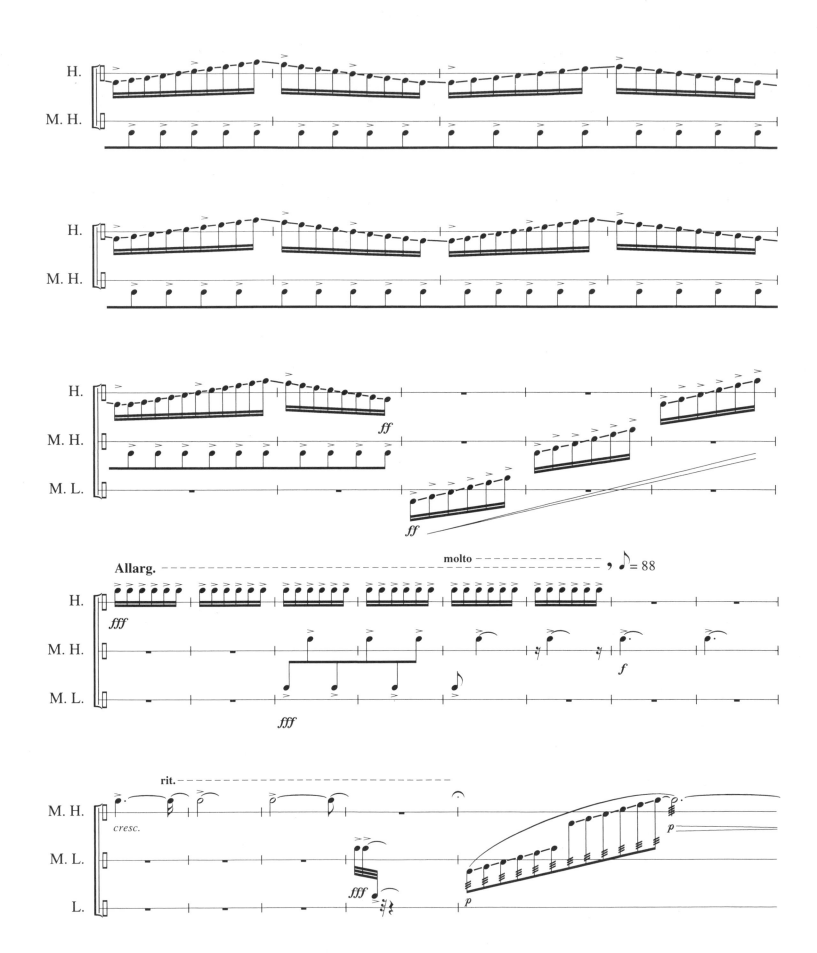

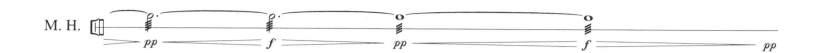

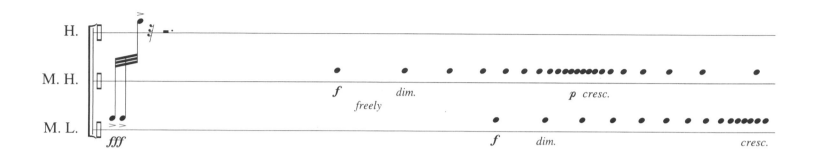

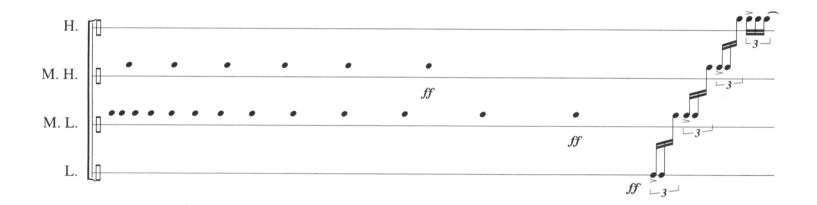

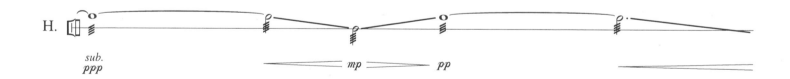

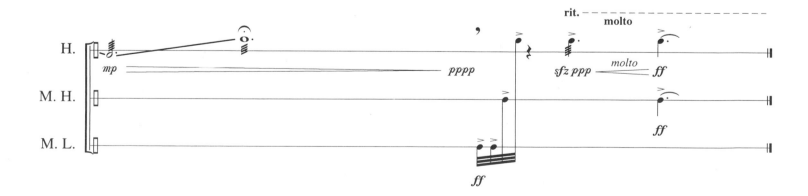

一柳 慧《リズム・グラデーション 》　　　　　●

ティンパニのための

初版発行─────────────────────1997年6月25日

第2版第3刷④───────────────2019年7月25日

発行─────────────────ショット・ミュージック株式会社

─────────────────東京都千代田区内神田1-10-1 平富ビル3階

─────────────────〒101-0047

─────────────────(03)6695-2450

─────────────────http://www.schottjapan.com

─────────────────ISBN 978-4-89066-404-7

─────────────────ISMN M-65001-018-4